# A COWBOY

---

# AT HEART

Wisdom, Wit & Poetry

# A COWBOY

for Cowpokes and

# AT HEART

Folks Who Love Them

## DAVID KOPP

MULTNOMAH BOOKS

SISTERS, OREGON

A COWBOY AT HEART

published by Multnomah Books

a part of the Questar publishing family

© 1997 by David Kopp

International Standard Book Number: 1-57673-088-3

Design by D2 Design Works

Printed in the United States of America

Scripture quotations are from the New International Version  (NIV)

© 1973, 1984 by International Bible Society

used by permission of Zondervan Publishing House

For information:

Questar Publishers, Inc.

Post Office Box 1720

Sisters, Oregon  97759


Library of Congress Cataloging-in-Publication Data

Cowboy at heart/ by Questar Publishers
        p.   cm
    ISBN 1-57673-088-3 (alk. paper)
    1.  Cowboys—West  (U.S.)—Miscellanea. 2. West  (U.S.)-
Miscellanea.    I. Questar Publishers
F596.C872        1997
978'.0088'636—dc21
                                                    97-3833

                                    CIP

97  98  99  00   01   02   03   04   05 — 10   9   8   7   6   5   4   3   2   1

# Contents

*Special thanks to:*

*Dean Rea for your skillful help in interviewing,*

*Katherine Hillis for your care with a million details,*

*and the working cowboys who took*

*the time to talk with us.*

Cowboys like to say that every man chooses his wages. So, they say, choose the big payoff—like spending your days on horseback under God's wide heaven. The money ain't there, but the payoff sure does make up for it.

A cowboy will tell you if you're doing your job, and doing it in the right place on earth, even the dust there will have your name on it. And when you turn in at night, you'll find gold in your pockets.

Maybe that way of thinking is what makes the American cowboy our most enduring hero—underpaid, sleep-deprived, bone-jarred, and dust-covered as he's always been. Heroes or not, they come riding into our little town (population 860) every June for the Professional Rodeo Cowboys Association rodeo. It's the one time of the year when rodeo athlete, ranch hand, and city dude all stand around wearing the same hats, kicking the same dirt.

This little book is for the cowboy heart in all of us—maybe especially for the average guy who can't seem to shake loose of lone prairie thoughts in a parking lot world. It's for people who:

- long for simple things

- enjoy living close to nature—or wish they only could

- think a horse holds up his end of a conversation just fine

- still value courage, honor, hard work, and sudden humor in bad circumstances, and

- sustain a genuine faith in the Lord above.

It's a book about cowboys, just ordinary people after all, who wouldn't take a million for their saddlebags of dreams. Set yourself down for a spell. Maybe you're one of 'em.

—DAVID KOPP
SISTERS, OREGON

## There's Peace in Simple Things

------------------------------------------------------------

The cowboy way of life starts with a wide sky, a good horse, a hard day's work, and a few simple passions. 〜 Out West, a man doesn't want things complicated. This is the country where, like one cowboy said, "there are more cows and less butter, more rivers and less water, and you can see farther and see less than any country in the world." 〜 Any cowboy knows you gotta slow down if you want to get there faster. 〜 So pull on your boots, and pick up your saddle. There's peace in simple things. The country up ahead is what cowboys call "the big high 'n lonesome," and it's waiting.

"A HEART AT PEACE GIVES LIFE TO THE BODY." —PROVERBS 14:30

- - - - - - - - - - - - - - - - - - - - - - - - - - - - - - - - - - - - - - - - - - - - -

## Part of Something Grand

"I like to see cattle being driven and horses being moved, and I like to see that dust boiling up. I like to smell mesquite smoke around the chuckwagon or around the branding pen. I guess it makes me feel that I'm a part of something in this old world."

—A TEXAS RANCHER

## Black Coffee Before Dawn

"The dark yard in front of the house is parked full of pickups. Restless horses that were saddled by starlight over an hour ago snort and shift against the sides of the close trailers. Men in spurs stomp up the steps to the door. They leave their big hats in a pile in the corner of the living room, nod at each other, and disappear into the kitchen to get a cup of coffee. They all drink it black. 'Spur juice,' one young puncher calls it, motioning for me to grab a cup."

—FROM IN THE KINGDOM OF GRASS, BY BOB ROSS

## A Happy Man

"I'm a happy man again. Dale is right next to me—and all I have to do is look through the window to see Old Trigger tied to a post."

—ROY ROGERS, 1949

## Little Things

I've laid for hours upon my back
Just looking at the sky,
At clouds, or if the sky was clear,
The motes within my eye.
D'ja ever spen' an hour or more
Just staring at the crick?
Or a scarab roll a ball of dung?
Or ants raslin' with a stick?
Or, on a cloudy, windy day,
See a windmill seem to fall?
Or stop stock still with neck
   hairs raised
By a plaintive coyote call?
Swallows slice their swaths across
The sky like scimitars.
I'm humbled by the intricate
Snowflakes' prismic stars.
I've laughed as stove-top killdeer
Go a-scrabblin' 'cross a draw.

I've seen cedar trees explode
   in flames
As I'm consumed with awe.

Arms crossed and leaning forward,
Weight on the saddle horn,
I'm a fascinated crowd of one;
A calf is being born.

The measure of your intellect,
The learn-ed people say,
Are the things that fascinate us.
They're a mental exposé.
You got to be dang careful
If you want to be thought smart,
And keep sorta confidential
Little things that's in your heart.

—WALLACE MCRAE, COWBOY POET,
RANCHER, FORSYTH, MONTANA

- - - - - - - - - - - - - - - - - - - - - - - - - - - - - - - - - - - - - - - - - - - - -

## Cowboy Fact

The average monthly wage for a cowboy in the 1880s was $35.

## God's Whopping Silence

"The highway went down into a narrow and immensely long, thunder-of-hooves valley, then like a chalk line, headed north, running between two low mountain ranges, the higher eastern one still in snow. A sign: NEXT GAS 80 MILES....

"Squat clumps of white sage, wet from a shower out of the western range, sweetened the air, and gulches had not yet emptied. Calm lay over the uncluttered openness, and a damp wind blew everything clean... there was no one. Listening, I walked into the scrub. The desert does its best talking at night, but on that spring evening it kept God's whopping silence; and that too is a desert voice.

"I've read that a naked eye can see six thousand stars in the hundred billion galaxies, but I couldn't believe it, what with the sky white with starlight. I saw a million stars with one eye and two million with both."

—FROM BLUE HIGHWAYS, BY WILLIAM LEAST HEAT MOON

## Cowpoke Horsesense

Go slow and get there quicker.

--------------------------------------------------------------

## Cowboy Lingo

*dally*—the full loop a roper takes around the saddle horn when the lasso is about to be tightened

*waddy*—cowboy

## 70 Years and an Old Pickup

A guest at a fancy Colorado dude ranch was trying to make conversation with Jack, a grizzled cowhand smoking his pipe on the porch. After a while, the guest asked, "Jack, do you ever feel like you've kind of wasted your life?"

Jack didn't say anything, and the guest kept talking. "All you've got to show for 70 years is that old pickup."

Jack just sat there, puffing on his pipe. Finally, he said, "Mister, all my life I've done for a living what you save up all year to do for two weeks."

## Cowboy Lingo

*chaparral*—thorny evergreen brush in the Southwest

*chaps, chappies*—leather pants or overalls, worn to protect a rider's legs from thorns or other injury

*Cowboy Close-up*

## Makin' Your Own Electricity

Bo and Kathy Lowe
China Creek Camp, Nevada

I f you telephone the "Bo" and Kathy Lowe family, expect to leave a message. They'll return your call when they get to town. And don't expect to follow electrical lines to their log cabin or to find school bus stops because they don't exist in this country where a ranch family may be 100 miles from the nearest neighbor.

Highway 93 trails north through Ely, Nevada, on to the Y that leads to Wells, crosses desert country and skirts the Salmon River to Jackpot near the Idaho border. To the west a family lives in what is known as China Creek Camp on the Y3 Ranch in high desert country.

"The closest place for groceries is a 50-mile trip one way," says Lowe. Because of the distance to school, their 17-year-old daughter Shawna is home-schooled.

Life in such a secluded spot is anything but lonesome or boring, Lowe says. "We ride until about time to go to bed. We play cards. Once in a while, we'll turn on the propane-powered generator, pop some popcorn, and watch a rented movie," he says. "Last night we had the generator on, Shawna played her electric guitar along with the radio, and we had a dance."

## Freezin'

"It got so derned cold at our ranch one winter that the thermometer dropped to ninety-five degrees below zero. Our foreman came out to give us orders fer the day, but the words froze as they came out of his mouth. We had to break 'em off one by one so's we could tell what he was sayin'."

—ANONYMOUS COWBOY, LIFE MAGAZINE, 1942

## Town for Sale (for those looking for room to grow)

Wagontire, Oregon
(between Burns and Alkali Lake on Highway 395)
population 2: Bill & Olgie Warner, owners
For $350,000 look what you get—
2 gas pumps
Cafe, post office, city hall, gift shop—a one-room building
8-unit motel
RV parking
Airstrip across the highway
Mule named Jack
& plenty of sagebrush to go around

## The Plainsman's Eye

"To leave behind all noise and mechanisms, and set out at ease, slowly, with one packhorse, into the wilderness, made me feel that I had found the ancient earth again after being lost among houses, customs, and restraints.

"I should arrive three days early at the forks—three days of margin seeming to me a wise precaution against delays unforeseen. If the Virginian were not there, good; I could fish and be happy. If he were there but not ready to start, good; I could still fish and be happy.

"And remembering my Eastern helplessness in the year when we had met first, I enjoyed thinking how I had come to be trusted. In those days I had not been allowed to go from the ranch for so much as an afternoon's ride unless tied to him by a string, so to speak; now I was crossing unmapped spaces with no guidance. The man who could do this was scarce any longer a 'tenderfoot.'

"My vision, as I rode, took in serenely the dim foothills—tomorrow's goal—and nearer in the vast wet plain the clump of cottonwoods, and still nearer my lodging for tonight with the dotted cattle round it.

"And now my horse neighed. I felt his gait freshen for the journey's end, and leaning to pat his neck I noticed his ears no longer slack and inattentive, but pointing forward to where food and rest awaited both of us. Twice he neighed, impatiently and long; and as he quickened his gait still more, the packhorse did the same, and I realized that there was about me still a spice of the tenderfoot: those dots were not cattle; they were horses.

---

## "If the Virginian were not there, good; I could fish and be happy. If he were there but not ready to start, good; I could still fish and be happy."

"My horse had put me in the wrong. He had known his kind from afar, and was hastening to them. When was I going to know, as by instinct, the different look of horses and cattle across some two or three miles of plain? The plainsman's eye was not yet mine, and I smiled a little as I rode."

—FROM THE CLASSIC WESTERN NOVEL, THE VIRGINIAN, BY OWEN WISTER

*Saddlebag Bible*

Better a dry crust with peace
than a house full of feasting
with strife.

—PROVERBS 17:1

-------------------------------------------------------------------

## A Psalm under Night Skies

O Lord, my Lord, your name is Awesome!
In created things I see your touch.
I hear your praise on the wind in the sage,
From bawlin' calves, and babies and such.

When I consider your night skies, God,
The moon and stars, all works of your fingers,
I wonder, what's a cowboy to you, Lord?
But you care 'bout me—and this thought lingers.

Somehow a broken down, busted cowpoke
Rates up with angels in your heavenly host.
You bless my days in the saddle, and make me
boss of your spread, from mountain to coast.

All cattle grazing the canyons are yours;
Every prairie hawk, rattler, or bobcat I see;
Every cuthroat leapin' the stream is yours, too—
Like me, alive by your blessing, wild 'n free.

O Lord, my Lord, your name is Awesome!
And it's comfortin' to know…you think about me!

—BASED ON **PSALM 8**, BY DAVID KOPP

## That's Why I'll Never Want to Be Anything But a Cowboy

In a myriad stars' light,
I ponder the night
And gaze on its splendorous treasure—
A beauty so rare,
just-a-hangin' up there.

The Lord did it all for my pleasure.
I awake with the dawn,
the thrill lingers on.
I bow, I worship with wonder....

That's why I'll never want to be
anything but a cowboy.

—FROM "THAT'S WHY I'LL NEVER WANT TO BE ANYTHING BUT A COWBOY,"
SONG LYRIC BY JACK HANNAH, OF THE SONS OF THE SAN JOAQUIN

## Cowpoke Horsesense

"Talk low, talk slow, and don't say too much."

—JOHN WAYNE

-------------------------------------------------------------

## *I Got to Go Out*

*What drives a man to duck out the door, or walk over the horizon?*

"Possibility is the oldest American story. Head west for freedom and the chance of inventing a spanking new life for yourself. Our citizens are always leaping the traces when their territory gets too small and cramped.

"Back in the late '50s, living with my wife and our small children in our little cattle-ranch house, when things would get too tight on a rainy Sunday afternoon in November, I always had the excuse of work. 'I got to go out,' I would say, and I would duck away to the peacefulness of driving the muddy fields and levee banks in my old Ford pickup....

"John Colter left Ohio at the age of 30, to head up the Missouri with Lewis and Clark in 1804. He stayed west another five years, earning his keep as a fur trapper in pursuit of beaver. One fearsome Montana winter he took a legendary walk from Fort Lisa on the Yellowstone, traveling through what is Yellowstone Park to circumnavigate the Tetons—about a thousand miles on snowshoes through country where no white man had ever been before. A thing both wondrous and powerful drove him. Maybe it was a need so simple as being out, away.

"Imagine those shining snowy mountains burning against the sheltering endless bowl of clean sky, and Colter alone there in Jackson Hole. We will not see such things again, not any of us, ever."

—FROM **OWNING IT ALL**, BY WILLIAM KITTREDGE, WESTERN AUTHOR, MISSOULA, MONTANA

## A Good Place to Think

"A person, worried by wars, inflation, taxes, and tormented by smog, noise, and the daily harassments of living, needs solitude to keep his sanity and perspective. The desert can supply it, though some find the desert too harsh. Here on Steens Mountain one can find both solitude and beauty. Winter is white and pure; spring comes late but is green and refreshing; summer is short and glorious; fall is often a display of riotous color. But solitude broods over the landscape. Weak men fear it and run back to the mob; strong men embrace it and learn; it weeds out the weaklings.

"Stand at the top of Steens Mountain, look far away into five states, look nearly straight down to the beautiful Alvord Ranch, then look carefully around at the alpine wild flowers. Try to take the time to sit down and watch how sunshine and shadow first color, then wipe out and recolor the scene. This is a good place to think about America for a few hours.

"Maybe this is what our mountain has to offer: enduring beauty, quiet, and blessed solitude. Those things aren't listed among the seven thousand items in a supermarket. Here the poorest may purchase as much as the richest."

—FROM **STEENS MOUNTAIN**, BY E.R. JACKMAN AND JOHN SCHARFF

-----------------------------------------------------------------

*Cowboy Close-up*

### It's All I Ever Wanted....
*After 50 years, the high country still calls*

Wilbur Plaugher: rancher, rodeo clown
Sanger, California

When he was a teenager back in the '40s, Wilbur Plaugher discovered the life he really wanted—and he's never changed his mind. "I got to go on cattle drives in the High Sierras and I thought that was the only life there was. I would stay back in the high country all summer, sleep out, pack out to get supplies. I'd look after cattle, rain or snow or shine. My hands would get so cold in the snow I couldn't unbuckle my chaps. But I still liked it."

Today, Plaugher is one of rodeo's best-known clowns. And he still works 10- or 12-hour days running cattle on 18,000 acres of mostly leased land in the Sierras. Getting away to a rodeo to clown is his idea of relaxing. "Cowboying, rodeoing, riding broncs and bulls is my entire life. It's all I ever wanted.

"It takes as much knowledge to be a great cowboy as any skilled laborer, although it probably has the lowest pay," he says. "You do it because you like to feel a good horse between your legs. You like riding and feeling the cool breeze. There's nobody, no city, no smog. You're driving cattle and living in nature.

"It's a wonderful way of life."

## Driftin' On

I had money in my pocket, my clothes were new
    I could do whatever I wanted to;
I was free as the wind that strummed the night stars
    Like the strings of a cowboy's old guitar.
Waitin' to meet each new dawn,
    Just a cowboy driftin' on.

—FROM "DRIFTIN' ON," BY EVERETT G. JONES, COWBOY, ELLENSBURG, WASHINGTON

------------------------------------

ord,

it's a crazy and wonderful world,

with a thousand distractions.

Help me to hold on tight to the few things

in life that really matter.

Give me your strength to make the simple

but tough choices. And fill my

cowboy heart with peace along the trail.

Amen.

## Real Cowboys Wear Dust

-------------------------------------------------------

**T**he hired man on horseback first rode out onto the open ranges of Texas in the 1860s. He developed a sixth sense for animal well-being, a fearless grace in the saddle, and a memorable style of dress. Within 30 years, the heyday of the cowboy was over, and he rode into American legend. But not into the past. Ranges may be fenced and Dodge City quiet on Saturday night, but cowboying is still part of life out West. You can still judge a man by the set of his hat or the braid of his lasso. And, for every man who makes his living on a horse, a thousand savor that life in their hearts. Like one Nevada man says, "What I do for a paycheck is computer systems analysis—who I am in my heart is a cowboy."

MAN LOOKS AT THE OUTWARD APPEARANCE, BUT THE LORD

LOOKS AT THE HEART. —1 SAMUEL 16:7

-------------------------------------------------------------

## That's What a Cowboy Is...

*A cowboy sets down the basics of his profession*

"A cowboy is a man a' horseback. And all down through history people have always looked up to a man on horseback....

"A cowboy, number one, right up front, has got to be a stockman. That's what a cowboy is. There's a 'cow' in a 'cowboy.' You gotta be able to look at a cow and know if she's healthy. You gotta be able to look at her coat, her hide, and tell if she's on good feed. You gotta be able to look in her eyes and tell if she's in trouble of any kind. You gotta be able to look at a calf and tell if that calf has sucked today or if he's lost his mother.

**"I use a rope twenty times a day;**

**I've used a gun twice."**

"Ridin' a horse is basic. You ride a horse to git from one place to another. And you gotta be able to rope. That's an important thing. Movies emphasize gunplay, but a rope is the most important tool to a cowboy. I use a rope twenty times a day; I've used a gun twice, to put a cow out of her misery."

—TOM BRYANT, COWBOY, BIG HOLE, MONTANA
FROM **OUT WEST**, BY DAYTON DUNCAN

--------------------------------------------------------------

## Cowpoke Horsesense

Rule #1 for personal safety in cow country:
Don't mess with a man's hat!

## What to Call a Cowboy

*It all depends…*

The look and name of cowboying varies throughout the West. Long-time cowboys can tell immediately where a man is from by his dress, his gear, his language, or how he goes about his work.

How you might address a cowboy breaks down by three main regions: buckaroos (Oregon, Nevada, Idaho, and California), cowpunchers (Texas, Oklahoma, New Mexico, and Arizona), and cowboys (Montana, Wyoming, Colorado, the Dakotas, Nebraska, and Canada). But a cowboy anywhere is just as likely to refer to himself as a puncher, hand, cowhand, waddy, or wrangler, among many other names. Generally, a cowman, stockman, or rancher describes an owner or manager, not a hired hand.

The name buckaroo probably evolved from the Spanish *vaquero*, meaning "cow worker." Cowboy is a literal translation of the same word. The term cowpunching came from the job of loading, or punching, cattle up into rail cars at the trailheads in the 1880s.

--------------------------------------------------------------

## Full Tilt on Sugar Lips

*A tenderfoot's account of rapid transportation*

"Still climbing, we follow the creek into thicker timber of straight and tall ponderosa pine, yellow and brown trunks with high, green branches that shade us from the sun. The temperature drops and the noise hits a crescendo when we cross the creek on a log bridge, then we round a ridge and the sound of the water is gone as quickly as it first reached us. Indian paintbrush and lupine begin decorating the trail in the pines. Through the occasional breaks in the trees, the snow-capped mountain peaks tower above us—white substitutes for the clouds that are missing. A narrow irrigation ditch courses next to our path....

"The horses stop to slurp the irrigation water. Bernstein says we'll leave the trail here to angle over to a high meadow a half-hour away. He and Winsome turn down the steep side of the ditch and disappear into the ponderosas; Sugar Lips is still slurping. After several kicks in her side, I wheel her around to follow down the embankment.

"What happens next is a blur in my memory, recalled in sensations of color, sound, and motion, and then pain. As soon as Sugar Lips reaches the bottom of the embankment, her ears go straight back and she lunges into a full gallop. Not a trot, not a canter. A full-steam gallop through the trees.

"These things I remember: pulling the reins and saying 'Whoa!' to no effect; gold shafts of sunlight and dark green shade; lighter green branches slapping my face; Joel's voice shouting something unintelligible as Sugar Lips and

REAL COWBOYS WEAR DUST

---

## "As soon as Sugar Lips reaches the bottom of the embankment, her ears go straight back and she lunges into a full-steam gallop through the trees."

I pass him and Winsome at careening, full tilt; losing my Stetson to the force of rushing air, a branch, a bounce, something; and the yellow-brown trunks of ponderosas, particularly those tree trunks, telescoping to the size of brick columns as we weave through them until it seems we're running through a solid maze of yellow-brown.

"Somewhere along this route, I fall off Sugar Lips' left side, spread-eagling and turning, my arm and face scraping dry pine from the ground cover. My right knee strikes something hard, sending a pulse of bright color through my mind. I roll two or three times and come to a stop next to a tree. It's a yellow and brown ponderosa.

"Joel trots up, carrying my hat. He sees I'm alive and trots on through the trees. A few minutes later he reappears with Sugar Lips in tow. Horse and hat are uninjured.

"'Can you stand up?' he asks, handing me my hat."

—FROM OUT WEST, BY DAYTON DUNCAN

---

--------------------------------------------------------------------

## Cowboy Lingo

*tenderfoot*—a term first applied to plains cattle that got sore-footed when they were brought west into rockier terrain. Later applied to Eastern newcomers who were trying to become working cowboys

*dude*—a city person out in cowboy country for recreation only

## Cowboy Fact

### The Stetson Story

In 1865, John Stetson opened a one-person hat factory in Philadelphia. After a trip west, he designed a hat that copied the style he had seen worn in Colorado. His design became synonymous with the cowboy look, and made Stetson a millionaire. A devout Baptist, John Stetson gave generously to churches and charities.

The word Stetson came to mean a hat, whether of that brand or another.

Many a cowboy spent a first paycheck on a Stetson, got married in a new one, or buried in an old one. Cowboys swore by the durability of Stetsons. Western folklorist Rick Steber tells the story of two outlaws who were executed in Weeksville, Montana, in 1882 and buried with their Stetsons. When the remains were disinterred 42 years later, the hats were still recognizable.

## Resist All

Now I see lots of dudes in town,
Wearing ball hats without any crown.
Some of them with the pretty curls,
Go bare-headed just for the girls.

But to me a cowboy is judged by his hat.
Whether he's tall and thin or short and fat.
If his hat isn't bent from pullin' it down,
You'll know he's a pickup-drivin' city clown.

Until it's weathered and shaped to fit,
A hat isn't worth a handful of grit.
It's when it becomes a part of your head,
It's a hat when you forget and wear it to bed.

—J'WAYNE "MAC" MCARTHUR, COWBOY POET, HORSE SHOW JUDGE
LOGAN, UTAH

------------------------------------------------------------

## Minimum Ranching Requirements

*(or what it takes to be a genuine cowman)*

1. A wide-brimmed hat, one pair of tight jeans, and $20 boots.

2. At least two head of livestock, preferably cattle—one male and one female.

3. A new air-conditioned pickup with automatic transmission, power steering, and trailer hitch. A second-hand car for going out to feed the cows when your wife borrows the pickup.

4. A gun rack from the rear window of the pickup, big enough to hold a walking stick and rope.

5. Two dogs to ride in the bed of the pickup truck.

6. A $40 horse and $300 saddle.

7. A gooseneck trailer, small enough to park in front of the cafe.

8. A little place to keep the cows, on land too poor to grow crops.

9. A spool of barbed wire, three cedar posts, and a bale of prairie hay to haul around in the truck all day.

10. Credit at the First National Bank, the feed store, and the vet.

11. A good neighbor to feed the dogs and cattle whenever you're gone fishing or hunting.

12. A pair of silver spurs to wear to barbecues.

13. A rubber cushion to sit on for four hours at the auction ring every Friday.

14. A good pocketknife, suitable for whittling to pass away the time at the sale barn.

15. A good wife who won't get upset when you walk across the living room with manure on your boots. Best if she has a full-time job teaching school.

## Cowboy Boot Facts

• The pointed toe helps the boot slide into the stirrup, and the high arch and heel keeps the boot from slipping through. The thin sole helps the cowboy feel the horse.

• A cowboy boot is made for riding, not walking. Calf ropers who must be nimble on foot in the arena wear flat-heeled boots.

• Ornamentation on boots originated with Mexican vaqueros who decorated boots with inlaid silver, finely stamped leather, and coins.

• Justin brand bootmakers of Fort Worth, Texas, has been in operation since 1879.

-----------------------------------------------------------

*Cowboy Close-up*

## A Place to Call Home

Larry Schutte, cow boss
Wells, Nevada

F or most of his 42 years, Larry Schutte was a cowboy looking for a place to throw down his bedroll. He moved a lot while learning the cattle business, he says.

"I went to a lot of places in Nevada just to see what this country was like. Seems like God makes certain people for certain country, and this fits me. I like the drier climate. It's a place where a cow can use her own teeth to make a livin' for you. But that's personal. A lot of people see what I see and say that this is nothin'."

Three years ago, Schutte, his wife Toni, and their two children found that place—a 350,000-acre ranch they lease near Wells, Nevada.

The Big Springs Ranch doesn't have a lot of roads running through it, other than Interstate 80. Schutte's crews may take five or six extra horses with them while working the ranch's rugged areas. "You have to have something as a backup," he says. "If you're riding young horses, you had better have lots of them."

When Schutte and his family moved onto the Big Springs Ranch, they knew it would mean more work than romance. Schutte works what he calls "28-hour days." Each morning from September to July he puts on worn-out long johns. Then it's Wrangler jeans, a hand-me-down shirt, and a pair of boots.

**"Seems like God makes certain people for certain country, and this fits me. It's a place where a cow can use her own teeth to make a livin' for you."**

He admits to owning a new "silver belly" hat that he received as a gift. And he'll dress up in a new shirt on special occasions. "I'm not picky," he says. "I don't care what I wear. Most cowmen in the country have a nice clean colored shirt. There's not too many extravagant people in northern Nevada."

Schutte is not looking for a new horizon these days. All the horizon he wants comes to his door. "We have a window in our bedroom that's about 8 by 10. We can wake up in the morning and see the whole country right there, out of that window."

## Cowboy Fact

A working cowboy can wear out a saddle every seven or eight years. When you order a new one from the better saddle makers, you're likely to wait a year to take delivery.

## Cowboy Hat Facts

- A cowboy shapes a new hat over a steaming kettle. Steam softens the felt. Each cowboy wants a custom look, or the look that's regionally favored.

- A cowboy never puts his hat brim-down on a surface. Protecting the customized shape of the brim is of utmost importance. If his hat isn't on, the cowboy's probably in bed, in the shower, or at a funeral.

- "Ten gallon hat" referred to a hat with a very high crown.

## Baby Say, "Horse..."

"The first word my mother can remember me saying was 'horse.' I've always been around horses, cows, and cowboys. When I was a kid I would hide my shoes and wear my boots. I was always hanging around that stuff."

—GREGG MCDONALD, SADDLE SHOP OWNER, WEISER, IDAHO

## The Fine Art of Braiding Rawhide

*Cowboying in the West and Southwest was strongly influenced by the Spanish heritage of Old California and the Mexican vaquero. Here an admiring cowboy describes the vaquero's artristy with a rope.*

"These California vaqueros were wonderful with livestock, from one end to the other. They were absolute experts at the art of braiding rawhide. They would plaid long lasso ropes with a rawhide honda, so the rope would slide through easily. These were called reatas, and were sometimes 70 feet long. They made rawhide bridle reins with a long rawhide romal with a leather snapper on the end, and they braided hackamores with a light headstall attached. This getup was very effective in handling young, green horses.

"There was one particularly beautiful rope made out of different colors of horsehair, called a McCarty. The McCarty was fashioned about the Turk's head on the nosepiece, or bosal, of the hackamore. It was so fashioned that the pressure was on a green horse's nose and jaw.

"The reatas were greased lightly with a cow's bag or oiled with unsalted butter, to keep them pliable and in shape. When the vaquero caught an animal with his rawhide reata, he would take two or three turns on his big saddle horn. The big horn cap would hold his rope, and the cap below was built up enough to hold his turns. After he had roped one or two animals and taken these hard, tight turns, his rawhide rope would begin to make grooves in the latigo leather of his saddle horn. Soon the reata would fit neatly into these grooves, almost by itself."

—EMMET WHITE, COWBOY, EARLY 1900s, JOHN DAY COUNTRY, OREGON

------------------------------------------------------------

## Cowpoke Horsesense

If the saddle creaks, it's not paid for.

## The Bear End of a Rope

"I have caught some unusual animals with a lasso, and have killed numerous rattlesnakes with the honda end of a rope. I have known men to rope coyotes with a reata, which can be pretty exciting. If caught in an open space, Mr. Coyote will ring his tail, hang out his tongue, and not make much speed toward getting away, because he is so scared.

"A rancher on Cottonwood Creek, Lime Swick, told me he caught a yearling bear one time on a big flat in the mountains. After a lot of trouble with his horse, Lime got near enough to the bear to get a loop on his hind leg and bring him into the ranch. His horse was not too happy about it."

—EMMET WHITE, COWBOY, EARLY 1900s,
JOHN DAY RIVER COUNTRY, EASTERN OREGON

## Cowboy Lingo

*chinks*—short chaps worn in hot country

*chuck*—food, carried in the chuck wagon

## Saddlebag Bible

"Do you see a cowhand skilled in his work?
He will ride for the big spreads—
he'll never be stranded on a broken-down horse
in a shirt-tail outfit."

—PROVERBS 22:29, COWBOY PARAPHRASE

## Cowboy Fact

*The Gun That Won the West:*

The 1873 Winchester, .44-40, center-fire, repeating rifle was designed by John Browning for Oliver Winchester's manufacturing company. The '73 Winchester became known as "the gun that won the West." Cowboys liked it because ammunition was interchangeable with revolvers. The '73 was preceded by the popular 1866 "Yellow Belly" Winchester—a gun with bronzed chamber coverings.

## Never Give a Necktie to a Cowboy

### Do's and Don'ts for Making a Cowboy Smile

| COWBOYS LIKE | COWBOYS DISLIKE |
| --- | --- |
| cattle | sheep |
| bandanas, or bolo ties | neckties |
| shirts with snaps | shirts with buttons |
| black hats | white T-shirts |
| bay horses | white horses |
| Wrangler jeans | any other jeans |
| Olathe boots | sandals |
| Stetson hats | baseball caps |
| pickups | bicycles |
| well-oiled hunting rifles | well-oiled politicians |
| cowgirls | fraternity boys |
| middle of nowhere | downtown anywhere |
| Allan Jackson | Michael Jackson |
| a buckle that he won | a buckle that makes him look like he won |

## Saddlebag Bible

Finish your outdoor work
and get your fields ready;
after that, build your house.

—PROVERBS 24:27

## Cowpoke Horsesense

Tossing your rope before building a loop
won't nearly catch you a calf.

*Cowboy Close-up*

### Always Been A-Horseback....
*You want to live long and happy? Be "honest tough," says this old-timer—and keep ridin'.*

Frank W. "Hank" McLees, cowboy
Cheyenne, Wyoming

When Hank McLees started riding and roping as a boy, Woodrow Wilson was president. The nearest fence was 50 miles away. A car was just a fancy horse buggy.

But today Hank's in good health because, he says, he's "always been a-horseback." At 86, he still rides. And he can still roll out clear, colorful stories of the Old West like it was—and like it remains in memory.

Frank W. "Hank" McLees grew up on a homestead at Campstool, Colorado, 23 miles south of Cheyenne. "My father had about 300 head of cattle and 40 head of good horses, which were worth a lot of money in them days. That's what they depended on. The Model T hadn't come in yet," says Hank.

By the time he was 10, McLees was spending weeks at a time on roundups and brandings. He'd rope and bring the çalves in while two cowboys branded. As many as fifteen to eighteen cowboys worked the drives and the branding. "They didn't know how to read or write," McLees says, "but they sure had an education in stock."

Any mistakes could be paid for in blood—the cattle back then were still Longhorns, which McLees says "could really rake you." "You had to be a rough, tough character to be a cowboy. Not mean, just honest tough. You gonna ride an old horse for ten to twelve hours, you better be tough."

In true cowboy tradition, Young Hank learned to mix mindfulness with bravado. He recalls an incident when he was about 18 and had been riding all day in the cold. When he arrived at camp, other cowboys were crowded around the potbellied stove, keeping warm and telling stories.

"There wasn't any place to sit," McLees says. "So I got a handful of .22 bullets and dropped them over their heads on the stove. "I ducked and boy did they scatter. The bullets went ping, ping. I knew how many bullets I had put on the stove. When the last one went off, I had all kinds of room next to the stove."

He spends his time these days on a five-acre ranch south of Cheyenne. "I've got two good horses out in the corral that I ride once in a while," he says. "I'm too old to cowboy, but I can still get on a horse better than some of these 18-year-olds."

**"You had to be a rough, tough character to be a cowboy. You gonna ride an old horse for ten to twelve hours, you better be tough."**

------------------------------

ord,

*you didn't make me a fancy,*

*uptown kind of person.*

*But no matter what I look like*

*on the outside, I want to have*

*the heart of a true cowboy—*

*real as dust—through and through.*

*Bless the work of my hands and*

*the sweat of my brow.*

*And guide me in your way.*

Amen.

## Get on Yer Horse 'n Ride

---

**Y**ou can't hide when you're on horseback. Whether you're a working wrangler or a bronc rider, you put what you know about animals in the saddle every day. Your savvy is always showing—or you're probably eatin' dirt. The test might come in a corral in Oklahoma or under rodeo lights in Bakersfield. And what might look like meanness to critters is more likely just fun all 'round and a natural kind of understanding. You know you have it, says one cowboy, if "you've got a disposition that makes you wanna get on a horse and ride all day." A cowboy knows that a horse is his partner, a good cow dog is his friend, and livestock are money in his purse. If you take care of them, they just might earn you the life you really want.

"A RIGHTEOUS MAN CARES FOR THE NEEDS OF HIS ANIMAL...."

—PROVERBS 12:10

## Love At First Ride

"It sure helps if you know you've got a good horse. The first time I met Trigger, I wanted to know how good a horse he was, so I got on him and turned him. Well, he could spin on a dime and give you nine cents back in change. We just fell in love. From then on, I never let him out of my sight. Finding a horse like Trigger is like finding a wife. The horse is your other half in this—he's your partner, and he can get you out of plenty of scrapes and close calls."

—ROY ROGERS

## Looking Down on the Hayloft

"Horses have played an important part in my life since I was a colt myself. Many times I've been on a horse when I went up but there was no horse there when I came down. Some bucked so high I could look down into the hayloft. I've been bitten, kicked, struck, stepped on, run away with, treed on the corral fence, and had horses fall on me, but I still like horses."

—WALTER SCOTT, COWBOY, EARLY 1900s, EASTERN OREGON

## Cowboy Fact

Cattle drive better into the wind.

## Cowboy Facts

The Quarter Horse Story
*from cow pony to legend*

The cow pony of choice for a hundred years has been the sturdy quarter horse, originating in the colonial states where it was bred first for work, then for racing the quarter mile (hence the name). A quarter horse profile is instantly recognizable—compact body, sloped shoulders, well-muscled hindquarters, and powerful, wide-set forelegs.

But it's the cow-smarts of the breed that means the most on the ranch. "A thoroughbred just has to move fast in a circle," says one cowboy. "But a quarter horse has gotta think, gotta watch where he puts his feet. He has to out-smart a cow and think right along with the buckaroo."

With two and a half million registered entries with the American Quarter Horse Association, you can understand why lots of folks think the "cow pony of choice" has become the most popular horse in the world.

## Cowboy Lingo

*catclaw*—a thorny tree common in the Southwest

*dogies*—calves generally, orphan or skinny calves in particular

## Buck to My Heart

*Many cowboys preferred a horse that bucked when first ridden. Will James used to call it "the right spirit at the right time." Another cowboy says, "I've always felt real close to a horse that had a lot of problems, I guess because I've always had some myself."*

"The next day I caught [Billy] up to ride and he showed me a thing or two. He started to buck, and first my six-shooter went, then my Winchester went, then I went, and he finished up by bucking the saddle over his head. After that I would not have taken a million dollars for him. He was about 10 years old when I got him, and was 36 years old when he died on this ranch of old age. He was a wonderful rope and cut horse, but I thought so much of him I never used him much, only to ride to town."

—E. C. "TEDDY BLUE" ABBOT, EARLY TEXAS COWBOY, REMEMBERS HIS FAVORITE HORSE, IN **WE POINTED THEM NORTH**

## Cowboy Fact

Rodeo riding events last up to eight seconds, but only half the points come from how well the cowboy rides—the other half come from how well the animal bucks.

## Cowpoke Horsesense

A good horse is never a bad color.

## A Horse of a Different Color

*appaloosa or palouse*—spotted horses descended from Nez Perce Indian war ponies

*bay*—reddish brown with black mane, tail, and points

*buckskin*—dusty yellow color of tanned deerhide

*chestnut*—various shades of gold

*dun*—yellowish, usually with different colored mane and tail

*flea-bitten*—brown flecks on a gray coat

*gray*—black skin with white and black hairs

*grulla*—mouse-colored

*paint, pinto*—patches of two colors, one being white

*palomino*—gold wheat-colored with white tale and mane

*roan*—white hair over black skin (blue roan) or brown skin (chestnut roan)

*sorrel*—reddish, with mane and tail of the same color; lighter color on legs

## The Stars and Stripes of Horse Markings

*blaze*—broader white mark down the forehead and over the muzzle
*bald face*—white on most of the head, past the eyes and surrounding the muzzle
*line-back*—dorsal marking down the center of a horse's back
*sock*—white anywhere up to the knee
*stocking*—white covers the knee
*star*—isolated white mark on upper forehead
*stripe*—narrow white mark down the forehead
*zebra markings*—stripes on legs; along with dorsal stripe, common in some bands of wild horses

## Reading a Horse's Mind

"I have studied horses and can read their minds very well, especially when they are homesick for their old range. No matter from which direction a horse is brought into an area, he knows the direction in which his home range lies. I have watched them many times. When you see a horse grab a few quick bites of grass, then raise his head and gaze intently toward his former home for a few moments, grab a few more bites, then gaze again, you'd better tie him up or, come morning, he will be gone."

—WALTER SCOTT, COWBOY, EARLY 1900s, EASTERN OREGON

---

## Cowpoke Horsesense

A man on foot is no man at all.

## On the Horns of History

*From the Longhorns of Texas to the steakhouses of today*

Longhorns, the original cattle of the trail drives after the Civil War, originated from stock brought to the New World by the Spanish. They roamed the open range in Texas by the millions in the 1860s. From 1865 to 1880, millions were driven north to cattle towns on rail lines in Kansas, Nebraska, and Wyoming. Longhorns were rangey, drought-resistant cattle able to withstand the rigors of the trail.

To produce more and better quality beef, other breeds have been introduced or crossed with Longhorns. Popular beef cattle these days include Charolais, Angus, Hereford, and various crossbreeds.

## Cowboy Fact

The widest recorded spread on a Texas Longhorn is 10 feet 6 inches.

## Wild Horses, Runnin' Free

*Call 'em Spanish barb, Indian mustang, or cowboy grief....*

Wild horses or mustangs descended from Spanish stock have roamed the West since the 1600s, when they came into common use by the Plains Indians. During the westward expansion of the 1800s, hundreds of runaway horses added to the feral herds.

Cowboys have traditionally hated wild horses because they compete for range with cattle, but ranches have also trapped wild horses for mounts, regularly releasing horses of higher quality to "breed up" nearby wild herds. But even hard-bitten cowhands will tell you that seeing a band of mustangs racing along a rimrock in the morning sun, shaggy manes and tails streaming, is one of life's finer moments.

These days, about 40,000 wild horses survive in the wild, mostly in Nevada. Herds on public lands are managed by the Federal Bureau of Land Management.

> **"Seeing a band of mustangs racing along a rimrock in the morning sun, shaggy manes and tales streaming, is one of life's finer moments."**

Some isolated regional herds, such as the Kiger Canyon mesteños, have maintained qualities of the original Spanish barb horse, and are highly prized by collectors.

Roundups, called gatherings, occur between August and early March, before foals are born and the weather turns warm. Captured horses are sold at auction. But helicopters have replaced horse and rider as the preferred way to bring in the herd, especially in rugged terrain.

"We use a helicopter along with a prather horse, also known as the Judas horse," explains one BLM staff person. "We place the horse in front of a trap area. The helicopter is used to locate and to move the wild horses toward the trap. As they near the Judas horse, the helicopter operator honks a horn and the horse is released. The Judas horse is trained to run to the trap and the wild horses follow."

*Cowboy Lingo*

*remuda*—the string of replacement horses a cowboy took with him on a roundup or cattle drive

*seago*—a lasso rope made of twisted hemp

--------------------------------------------------------------------

## Calf

Well, he's just a little feller.
Ain't yet got the strength to beller
And he's kind of wobbly legged at the knees.
He was born in a March blizzard,
Cold enough to freeze your gizzard,
But his mammy found 'im shelter in the trees.

Well, at first he don't know much,
But he savvies mammy's touch
And his teeter totter'n' get-up's plumb absurd.
Soon he gets the hang of walkin',
Learns his mammy's way of talkin'
So he'll know 'er from the far side of the herd.

He's bright-eyed as a camp robber
With his face all caked with slobber.
A feller'd have to say he's quite a mess.
But he's healthy and alert,
This rambunctious little squirt,
And his antics cause his mammy some distress.

He'll shore kick up quite a fuss,
This demandin' little cuss,
If his ma ain't there to feed 'im when it's time.
Soon he's racin' with the others,
Lots of them is his half-brothers,
Always lookin' for a bigger hill to climb.

All this cute's just incidental.
Naw, we don't get sentimental.
No sense a feller makin' lots of noise.
Ain't no need to sing or shout,
But he's what it's all about.
He's the lifeblood of the cattle country, boys.

—MIKE LOGAN, COWBOY POET, HELENA, MONTANA

*Cowboy Lingo*

*sawbones*—doctor

*stove up*—injured

## All the Fun Eight Seconds Can Buy

*Hold on to yer hat—let's rodeo!*

It's a crazy all-American sport that began when cowboys of the 1860s first had more time on their hands than sense. "To one who has never been on the back of a bucking broncho," a cowboy wrote home, "my advice is to try it if you have got the nerve, and you will in an instant find that a broncho is far different from the old family horse."

By 1882, promoter Buffalo Bill Cody figured he could charge admission, and his Wild West Show went on the road. Cowboys have been letting 'er rip ever since. Competitions are rooted both in regular ranch work (like roping steers) and pure challenge (riding bulls). Today, rodeo attracts sixteen million fans per year, and pros like Larry Mahan, Roy Cooper, and Ty Murray are nationally recognized pro athletes. The Professional Rodeo Cowboys Association (PRCA) regulates the rodeo circuit.

The major rodeo events are saddle bronc riding, bareback bronc riding, bull riding, steer wrestling, calf roping, team roping, and barrel racing.

The sport of cowboys can be hard on bones; bronc and bull riders rack up seventy-five percent of all rodeo injuries. But cowboys keep a positive outlook. One injured bull rider says of his bad luck, "I guess I must've been meek because I inherited a lot of earth."

## Most Common Rodeo Injuries

*Team roper:* missing finger
*Bronc and bareback rider:* knee, riding arm, flank strap lacerations to the back
*Bull rider:* getting gored by a horn

## Cowpoke Horsesense

A cowboy who says he's never been throwed ain't tellin' the entire truth.

## Rodeo Lingo

*rough stock*—bull riders, bareback, saddle bronc

*gristle head*—steer wrestler, bulldogger

*timeys*—calf and team ropers

## Cowboy Fact

The Brahma bull Red Rock threw 312 riders between 1980 and 1988 before he was finally ridden for the full eight seconds by world champion Lane Frost. A rodeo bull can weigh up to 2,200 pounds.

*Cowboy Close-up*

**Gettin' In, Gettin' Out—It Ain't Just for laughs....**

Wilbur Plaugher: bullfighter and rodeo clown
Sanger, California

When things get dangerous, the rodeo clowns and bullfighters get to work. Cowboys needed help keeping the bulls from trampling them, and the crowds liked the laughs.

Wilbur Plaugher, a veteran rodeo clown, has been turning away bulls and delighting audiences for more than three decades, and rodeoing for years before that.

"You learn how to be a clown and a bullfighter by experience," says Plaugher. Timing is everything. If it's off, you take home your lessons. "There hasn't been a place on me that hasn't been hooked by a bull," he says.

Riders know that a bullfighter's willingness to risk injury is what keeps him alive. "In bareback riding you have the pickup men to help the cowboy," Plaugher explains. "But the clown is the only thing a bull rider has. You watch

**"Timing is everything. If it's off, you take home your lessons."**

which hand the bull rider is riding with. You turn the bull the opposite way. That way the rider won't get bucked off the wrong way and get hung up."

The knack for timing is probably what keeps clowns and bullfighters wearing the same outfit, though some choose to do only one. At one time, Plaugher pulled a triple—competing in bulldogging finals as well as working as both a clown and bullfighter. After he turned 50, he stayed with clowning.

These days he takes nine or ten specialty acts to a rodeo. In true rodeo style, Plaugher loves extremes—in his acts, he's used trained goats, pigs, monkeys, dogs, and even chickens. "When you go from a timed event to a bucking event, there's always a minute or two," he says. "You get in there with your entertainment—and then you get out."

---------------------------------------------------------------

## How to Get a Horse in Your Pocket

### Training Tips from Ron Moore, Kerrville, Texas

"When God created the horse, he made himself a very complex animal. If you're trying to work a horse, you have to learn how to communicate with him in a way that he'll understand. Adam prob'ly knew how to understand animals perfectly, but the rest of us have to work at it.

"A horse isn't like a pickup. You can make a horse mad at you or like you. You can make him your friend or your enemy. Sometimes when I can't figure out how to solve a problem with a horse, I pray about it. I pray, 'Lord, show me somethin' more.' I'm saying that for serious. After all, you got a problem with a Ford, you go to Henry. You tryin' to figure out a horse, you go to his creator.

"There's two kinds of horses: the one that's trying to figure out what you want 'cause he wants to do it; and the one that, well, you pretty much have to make him do anything. By the way, sayin' an animal is spirited doesn't have anything to do with whether he wants to do what you want him to do. If your horse has a lot of energy, he's athletic, and he wants to please you—you got yourself one good animal.

"My starting rule for training a horse is pretty simple: apply the least amount of pressure required to get the response you want, then as soon you get your response, give instant relief from the pressure.

"Let's say you're trying to lead a horse. If you apply steady pull on the lead

## "If your horse has a lot of energy, he's athletic, and he wants to please you— you got yourself one good animal."

rope, you're just draggin' him. Same thing if you're trying to rein him. As soon as he moves the direction you want, release pressure. Pretty soon you'll have that horse right in your pocket.

"Another piece of advice: every motion of your hand should be supported by your leg. That way the horse learns to read your body.

"And never be rough with a horse that messes up—'cause he's tryin'. He's trying to figure it out, and remember you're teaching him the easiest way to do something. So he'll correct his mistakes. My kids taught me you can insist on what you know has to happen without getting rough. Like any good horse trainer will tell you, 'Always ask 'im nice!'"

## Cowboy Lingo

*honda*—sliding knot on the rope used to lasso

*reata*—a rope of braided leather or rawhide

## Saddlebag Bible

"Do you give the horse his strength
or clothe his neck with a flowing mane?
Do you make him leap like a locust,
striking terror with his proud snorting?
He paws fiercely, rejoicing in his strength,
and charges into the fray...."

—JOB 39:19-21

## Cowpoke Horsesense

Never get between a calf and its mother—if she's a good mother,
she's gonna charge you.

## Cowboy Fact

*Roping horse:* Quick, fast and smart, a roping horse is trained to keep the rope taut following the catch while the rider dismounts, then throws and ties the steer.

*Cutting horse:* Highly trained, a good cutting horse can separate one critter from the herd and maneuver it into a corner, anticipating every move of the cow and cutting off any undesirable breakout.

## The Smell of Money

"They shore ain't pretty and they don't smell good but there is somethin' 'bout a cow that makes the man that owns one feel like he's got money in his purse."

—SPIN LUCETTE, JENKINS, CALIFORNIA, 1869

## Cowboy Lingo

*bull rider*—rodeo competitor who rides bulls in timed events

*bullfighter*—rodeo gymnast and clown who keeps bulls from injuring fallen bull riders

## Cowpoke Horsesense

A poor hand on a good horse gets into more trouble than a poor hand on a poor horse.

## Cowboy Close-up

### That Special Feel for a Horse

*One professional horse trainer (and his cowdog, Will) have some tested advice about critters and life.*

Ron Moore, cutting horse trainer
Kerrville, Texas

Cowboy Ron Moore owes a lifetime of professional success to his way with a horse. Moore grew up on horses—"ranch raised," he calls it—won a scholarship that took him through college as a champion saddle bronc rider, and spent years on the PRCA rodeo circuit. Today he's a professional horse trainer in Kerrville, Texas.

"Everyone wants to get on a horse for some reason," he says. "But most people ride for an hour or so, and that's enough. But if you're made to be a cowboy, you've got a disposition that makes you wanna get on a horse and ride all day. When I was working ranches in Colorado, I was on a horseback for three months at a stretch—twelve hours a day, six days a week, day after day, horse after horse. To me, that was livin'."

Moore now breaks colts and trains high-quality cutting horses for a living. A cutting horse is trained to separate out a cow from the herd, following only leg signals from the rider. Training a skilled, competitive cutting horse requires huge amounts of patience and experience, and what Moore calls "that special feel for a horse."

-------------------------------------------------------------

**"If you're made to be a cowboy, you've got a disposition that makes you wanna get on a horse and ride all day."**

Moore owes his most recent "professional" venture to his cowdog, Will, an Australian Blue Heeler. "Every Sunday morning we'd find him in the pickup, ready to go," Ron says. His church-minded dog got him thinking about his faith and the cowboy life. Next thing you know, Moore was reading a poem he wrote about Will for an enthusiastic audience. It only seemed natural to have Will on the stage too.

Weekdays it's still horses from dawn to dark for Cowboy Ron and Cowdog Will, but weekends often find the pair on the road. "Will sits next to me on a bale of hay. If there's no hay around, he doesn't mind using a chair. Sometimes he'll tell jokes, and I pick my guitar.

"If I ask him to tell the audience his favorite verse, he'll get up and whisper in my ear," says Moore. "So I tell folks what he said: 'Resist the devil, and you won't have fleas!' Will never gets that verse right."

## Get On Yer Horse 'n Ride

-------------------------------

ord,

*at work or at play in your world,*

*may I see your goodness*

*all around me—in people, in critters,*

*in everything you've made.*

*Draw me to you in the deepest part*

*of my cowboy heart.*

*And when the riding gets rough,*

*help me trust in you—*

*and let 'er buck!*

Amen.

*At Home on the Trail*

- - - - - - - - - - - - - - - - - - - - - - - - - - - - - - - - - - - - - - - - - - - - - - - - - - - -

**A**sleep after dark to the *yayeeeeee, yip, yip* of the coyotes. Awake before dawn to the bark of the cook, "Wake up, snakes, and bite a biscuit!" A cowboy's life during roundup or on the trail was missing nearly every comfort of home, yet was itself a home a cowboy could love. Weeks of branding mavericks or cutting steers tested endurances. Living and working under sun and stars gave him time to think about his Maker, and to wonder at God's creation. Riding lonely night herd gave him occasion to sing lullabies to nervous critters, or jot down poetry for a winter's campfire. Amidst the noise, dust, and sweat of the trail herd, the cowboy learned to hear the music of home.

## Just A-Ridin'!

Oh, for me a horse and saddle
Every day without a change;
With the desert sun a-blazin'
On a hundred miles o' range,

  Just a-ridin', just a-ridin',
  Desert ripplin' in the sun,
  Mountains blue along the skyline,
  I don't envy anyone.

When my feet are in the stirrups
And my horse is on the bust;
When his hoofs are flashin' lightnin'
From a golden cloud o' dust;
And the bawlin' of the cattle
Is a-comin down the wind—
Oh, a finer life than ridin'
Would be mighty hard to find.

  Just a-ridin', just a-ridin',
  Splittin' long cracks in the air,
  Stirrin' up a baby cyclone,
  Rootin' up the prickly pear.

I don't need no art exhibits
When the sunset does his best,
Paintin' everlastin' glories
On the mountains of the West.
And your operas sound foolish
When the night bird starts his tune
And the desert's silver-mounted
By the kisses of the moon.

  Just a-ridin', just a-ridin'—
  I don't envy kings or czars
  When the coyotes down the valley
  Are a-singin' to the stars.

—A TRAIL SONG BY ELWOOD ADAMS,
COLORADO COWBOY, ABOUT 1908.

## How to Start—and Maybe Stop—a Stampede!

*A first hand description of an 1890s stampede*

"In trailing cattle to the railroad, great care is required in order to get them there in good condition. You must not hurry them to cause foot soreness; you must avoid having a stampede, if so your work for weeks may be thrown away.

"There are many ways which will cause a stampede. Perhaps when the cattle are herded together at night a thunderstorm will come up, and the heavy claps of thunder will terrify your stock, which will cause them to stampede in all directions. Then again the bark of a 'coyote' may start them, or, during the night some may become restless and in getting up tramp on those laying down. Then look out for trouble.

"It is on such occasions that our duty is of the most dangerous kind. We are obliged to ride after the cattle in the darkness, on our ponies, which have been hastily saddled, over usually a very rough country, not knowing what instant both you and your pony will go down into some hole.

"The boys ride on the outside of the herd, and by hitting them with our heavy whips and trying to get them to circle, if we are so fortunate as to do so, those cattle in the center are in time brought to a standstill, and the others, seeing those in the center stop, gradually get over their fright and halt also. Sometimes it is impossible to stop them, and the herd scatter in all directions, but few are lost, as they are recovered in the next roundup."

—L.F. FOSTER, COWBOY, 1890s

## Saddlebag Bible

He tends his herd like a skilled cowhand.
He gathers the calves in his arms,
and carries them close to his heart;
he gently leads those that are weak.

—ISAIAH 40:11, COWBOY PARAPHRASE

## Cowboy Lingo

*hackamore*—a bridle without a bit, easily made on the spot from rope

*hardtack*—hard, unleavened bread

## Old-Time Instructions for Brewing Trail Coffee

To two gallons of boiling water, add two pounds of coffee. Boil two hours, then throw a horseshoe into the pot. If it sinks, the coffee ain't done yet. Most coffee makers is too gen'rous with the water.

## Circle of Grub

*The chuck wagon was a world of comfort on wheels.*

Call it a restaurant on wheels, a rolling supply store, home away from home, or refuge from endless work—the chuck wagon was all of these and more. The chuck wagon, and its master, the cook, followed trail drives and roundups to keep cowboys fed and happy. Because of its importance, the cook wielded a lot of clout—second only to the trail boss. Says one historian, "Trail hands were at pains to stay in the cook's favor."

The circle around the chuck wagon was home base for weeks, and even months, at a time. Cowboys would roll out their bedrolls near it for sleep, then store the rolls in the wagon during the working hours.

The wagon carried water, flour, coffee, tools, firewood, bullets, and other essentials. Favorite meals were bacon and beans, biscuits, chili, steak, and "prairie oysters," the testicles of steer.

At mealtimes, on the ground next to the wagon, gathered the rough, sweaty crew that for more than one cowboy was the closest approximation to a family he might have during his working life.

## Five Horses and Twelve Miles of Cattle

*Unforgettable scenes from the trail*

"When I was ten I saw one of the last of the big drives, with over ten thousand head. I rode up on a high point with Sid Rogers to see the herd. He pointed out the long string, at least twelve miles of cattle, and said I had better take a good look—I might never see this sight again. Riders were there from every ranch for a hundred miles, just as they were in the 1880s.

"About this time I remember a roundup with four cook wagons at Benjamin Lake. There were three cow wagons and a horse outfit. The cooks wondered how many men they were feeding, so they counted the dirty plates after breakfast one morning. There were eighty-one.

"When men lined up in the morning, it looked about like the corrals at the Pendleton Roundup. Over five hundred horses were in the caviattas of the four groups. The men and horses combined to produce a colorful, action-filled sight. Some of the things you'd see—all going on at once—included:

Bucking horses.

Loose horses that had jerked away, maybe trailing a reata.

Horses losing their saddles.

Riders reaching for the ground.

Cowboys hobbling mean horses so as to saddle them without getting a hoof in the middle of breakfast.

Riders dashing around to catch horses.

Cooks serving the nighthawks.

But you wouldn't see much hilarity. This was all business."

—RUEB LONG, FROM THE OREGON DESERT

## Burnt Jes' Perfect!

*Kitchen rules at old-time cow camps*

"Know the rules in a cow camp when they have no regular cook. When any-body complains about the chuck they have to do the cooking. One cowboy broke a biscuit open and says, 'They are burnt on the bottom and the top and raw in the middle and salty as all-get-out, but shore fine, just the way I like 'em.'"

—ANONYMOUS, NEBRASKA PANHANDLE, 1880

## The World of the 1870s Cattle Drive

**13** "Boys, the secret of trailing cattle is never to let your herd know that they are under restraint," advised one early trail boss. To keep 3,000 to 5,000 head of cattle moving and under control took plenty of secrets, and weeks of nearly 'round the clock cowboying.

The job was simple and exhausting—"never let a cow take a step, except in the direction of its destination."

A trail herd of 3,000 head was favored as most manageable. Usually about ten cowboys, including the trail boss, or drover, were required to handle such a herd. Cowboys changed horses several times a day to keep from wearing out their animals. "Nighthawks"—teams of two cowboys—rode guard at night.

Government estimates show that between 1866 and 1885, 6 million cattle were trailed north from Texas, but some historians put the number as high as 9.8 million. The end of the great trail drive era came as a result of drought, barbed wire on the ranges, and changing market conditions.

## Cowpoke Horsesense

"Always ride a good horse—and breathe through your nose."

—A FATHER'S ADVICE TO A YOUNG COWBOY

## Hot 'n Howdy!

*Recipe for 1880s Texas Chili*

4 pounds coarse-cut or chopped meat
2 tablespoons fat or oil
1 chopped onion
5 or 6 minced garlic cloves
5 or 6 finely diced hot red or green chili peppers
2 to 4 tablespoons hot chili powder
Black or white pepper
1 quart spring water
1 tablespoon paprika
1 tablespoon crushed cumin seed
1 teaspoon Spanish oregano
1 teaspoon salt
1 teaspoon sugar
6 tablespoons flour
1 can tomato sauce
1 or 2 cans beans

--------------------------------------------------------

## How to Raise a Cowboy (from the Sack)

**Cowboy Gettin' up Hollers:**

"Rise and shine, and give God the glory."

"Grub pile!  Come a-runnin', boys!"

"Roll out there, fellers, and hear the little birdies sing their praises to God."

"Wake up, snakes, and bite a biscuit!"

"Bacon in the pan
Coffee in the pot
Get up an' get it
Eat it while it's hot!"


## Cowboy Quote

"Wandering men have always had a love for poetry, perhaps in part because it can be easily memorized and provides company on many a cold and lonely night."

—LOUIS L'AMOUR, WESTERN AUTHOR

## The Old Chisholm Trail

"Oh come along, boys, and listen to my tale,
I'll tell you all my troubles on the ol' Chis'm trail.

     Come a-ti yi youp youp ya youp yay,
     Come a-ti youp youp yay.

On a ten-dollar horse and a forty-dollar saddle,
I was ridin', and a-punchin' Texas cattle.

We left ol' Texas October twenty-third,
Drivin' up trail with a 2 U herd.

I'm up in the morning afore daylight,
An' afore I sleep the moon shines bright.

It's bacon and beans most every day,
I'd as soon be eatin' prairie hay."

—FROM "THE OLD CHISHOLM TRAIL," A TRADITIONAL COWBOY SONG

*Cowboy Close-up*

## Cow Camp Memories

*A Texan remembers no running water and a "real cowboy" father*

Jo Conatser
Trinity, Texas

J o Conatser grew up on the legendary Matador Ranch, the second largest ranch in the United States at the time it was sold in 1951. She remembers wide skys, red Panhandle dust, and the simplest of home amenities. More than that, she remembers with affection a tall, ramrod thin cowboy she called Dad.

Her father, Luther James "Slim" Felts, worked for the Matador for more than 30 years, running a "cow camp" covering thousands of acres. "They ranched a lot different back then," says Jo. "When the wagons pulled out in the spring, the cowboys pulled out too and stayed at the wagon. They'd work different areas around the Matador for weeks without coming back."

Established in 1878, the Matador stretched across much of the Texas Panhandle, with additional holdings in Montana and the Dakotas.

"I rode a lot while I was growing up," says Conatser, now of Trinity, Texas. "I was raised at one of the cow camps. The ranch furnished a house and groceries, but we were raised without running water, no bathrooms, no electricity."

---

## Her father's only cuss words were "swayed bellied son of a gun."

Everyone knew and respected her father. "Slim Felts was an excellent hand with horses. He rode the countryside on the ranch every morning. He was one of the best men that you could ever meet," she says.

"He had a lot of Indian in him. He didn't talk a lot, and I never heard him say anything bad about anybody. If he didn't like you, you didn't know it. If he told you something, that's the way it was. He didn't drink." Conatser says her father's only cuss words were "swayed bellied son of a gun."

"My dad didn't go to church very much," she says. "But I don't ever remember coming in when he was at home on a Sunday that he wasn't reading the Bible."

Her dad bulldogged a steer at age 65. Slim Felts died in 1980 when he was in his 80s. To the end, Conatser says, "he was a real cowboy."

- - - - - - - - - - - - - - - - - - - - - - - - - - - - - - - - - - - - - - - -

## Cowboy Quote

"I think of myself in the oral tradition—as a troubadour, a village taleteller, the man in the shadows of the campfire. That's the way I'd like to be remembered—as a storyteller. A good storyteller."

—LOUIS L'AMOUR, WESTERN WRITER, IN HIS AUTOBIOGRAPHY,
EDUCATION OF A WANDERING MAN

## That Rollin' Rhythm of the Range

"The poetry's in the rhythm of the horse—the walk, the trot, the lope. You kinda fall into the rhythm. If you hear something really good, it's because the meter is right and the rhythm is there. I figure my horse acts just like a metronome to a musician."

—JON BOWERMAN, COWBOY POET AND HORSE TRAINER, FOSSIL, OREGON

## Cowboy Fact

*Bedroll:* a tarpaulin large enough to contain a cowboy's blankets and personal possessions. During roundups or drives, cowboys' rolls were carried along in a wagon; a line rider tied his tightly rolled behind the saddle.

## Hard, Sweet Duties

"Getting up at three in the morning and trailing the cows all morning, that's fine. Then the sun comes up, you get hot, the flies start biting, and your horse is tired and you're tired. It gets old. It's just plumb work, but you still like it. You go up and down all day—you get second winds. You worry a lot about every little calf because we go so far. But by the end of the day, you're kind of proud of yourself."

—TARA MILLER, COWGIRL, BIG PINEY, WYOMING

## Cowboy Lingo

*beef tea*—shallow water stirred up by cattle

*brushpopping*—term used to describe searching through brush for cattle

- - - - - - - - - - - - - - - - - - - - - - - - - - - - - - - - - - - - - - - - -

## The West Came by the Porch Today

*If you keep a sharp eye, you just might see a bygone era at your front door.*

On this fine October afternoon, while a red-tailed hawk circles the meadow and the sun strikes gold in the aspen, we're sitting on the porch watching the West roll down the county road at the end of our driveway. About seventy-five head of cattle are bawlin' their way past our place, heading toward winter pasture.

Five cowboys and a pickup or two make sure the show keeps rolling.

One red calf doesn't feel inclined to roll. He feels inclined to straddle the yellow line on the asphalt for a spell and look back. In the left lane, a cement truck and a lady in a Suburban pull to a stop. The two cowboys riding drag and the calf's mother all move in to persuade the little critter to budge.

The calf lets go with a flood over the centerline while studying the cement truck. Then he decides to mosey in the right direction. By now most of the herd is strung out ahead, following the lead cow around the bend in the road. As if following a secret map, "Li'l Red" ambles straight for a hole in the barbed wire—probably the only one for miles—slides through, and heads toward the creek. The guy in the cement truck leans out his window. We think he's rootin' for the calf.

"We got one through the fence," Jackie growls into his walkie-talkie. He's the cowboy on the big dun, riding wing on our side of the procession. The lady drover on the other side, closest to the escaped critter, dismounts and walks out through the ponderosa to sweet-talk the little fella back to his kin. After considerable hat waving, she's gets the calf under the top strand and onto the road again.

---

**This afternoon if you squinted just
right through the dust, let the bawlin'
cattle and hollerin' cowboys fill your
ears..., you could still feel the real thing.**

We listen as Jackie encourages the cowboys riding drag to put on a little pressure, keep the cattle moving. "Don't want any more of 'em contemplatin' that hole in the fence," he says. Then the cement truck and the Suburban get the go-ahead, and they sidle past.

Too soon, only minutes it seems, the dusty river of cattle has dried up in the bend, the clatter of horse hooves has faded, and the last cowboy has ridden out of sight.

Our family doesn't live on the Chisholm Trail, just a no-place county road. But, this afternoon if you squinted just right through the dust, let the bawlin' cattle and hollerin' cowboys fill your ears, and hung onto the sharp, familiar smell of horse sweat on leather—you could still feel the real thing. The open range. The cowboy way. The crazy, kid urge to make a break for freedom. It was right there, hanging in the air like that old hawk.

—BY DAVID KOPP, SISTERS, OREGON

-----------------------------

ord,

*on this long ride through life,*

*I know that you are always with me.*

*You understand every craggy*

*range in my cowboy heart. And anywhere*

*I choose to go, you help me*

*feel at home there. May my words and*

*deeds bring honor to you, and goodness to*

*those who depend on me.*

Amen.

## *A Cowboy's Honor*

---

**T**he simple grave marker under the old juniper near here reads, "Cowboy, 17, Horse Kicked." No name. No family. No year. Just the manner of death, and the pride of occupation—"Cowboy." He wanted the freedom, thrill, and honest sweat of a cowboy's life—but his dream ended young. Maybe it is this daily nearness of danger and death that makes a cowboy demand a code of honor from himself and from those he depends on. When need arises, nothing less can be trusted. The code of the West meant being a man of your word, a protector of the weak, and a helping hand to strangers. And life—as always—was the best teacher.

"HE WHO GUARDS HIS WAY GUARDS HIS SOUL." —PROVERBS 16:17

--------------------------------------------------------------

## Those Who Do Not Fear to Die

"A man's usefulness depends upon his living up to his ideals insofar as he can. It is hard to fail but it is worse never to have tried to succeed. All daring and courage, all iron endurance of misfortune, make for a finer, nobler type of manhood. Only those are fit to live who do not fear to die, and none are fit to die who have shrunk from the joy of life and the duty of life."

—THEODORE ROOSEVELT, 26TH AMERICAN PRESIDENT,
FOUNDER OF THE ROUGH RIDERS

## What You Remember is What Changes You

Veteran cowboy Everett Jones, now in his 70s, still works his cattle near Ellensburg, Washington. He tells about the time in his boyhood when he broke his arm in a fall from a horse. He doesn't much remember the pain, just his father's oft-repeated advice: "Get up and try again."

## Cowboy Fact

Carved on a rock over a lone grave near Cripple Creek, Colorado:
> He Called
> Bill Smith
> A Liar.

----------------------------------------------------------------

## The Ten Commandments of the Cowboy

*This code, endorsed by Gene Autry and used for years by scout troups, describes the ethic of the working cowboy. Though simple (and certainly not always followed), such codes of honor made life on the frontier safer and more kindly.*

1.  A cowboy never takes unfair advantage—even of an enemy.
2.  A cowboy never goes back on his word.
3.  A cowboy always tells the truth.
4.  A cowboy is kind to small children.
5.  A cowboy is free from racial and religious prejudices.
6.  A cowboy is helpful to people in trouble.
7.  A cowboy is a good worker.
8.  A cowboy neither drinks nor smokes.
9.  A cowboy respects womanhood, his parents, and the laws of his country.
10. A cowboy is a patriot.

- - - - - - - - - - - - - - - - - - - - - - - - - - - - - - - - - - - - - - - -

## Drifting Down the Years

"The men and women who lived the pioneer life did not suddenly disappear; they drifted down the years, a rugged proud people who had met adversity and survived. Once, many years later, I was asked in a television interview what was the one quality that distinguished them, and I did not come up with the answer I wanted. Later, when I was in the hotel alone, it came to me.

"Dignity."

—LOUIS L'AMOUR, WESTERN WRITER, IN HIS AUTOBIOGRAPHY,
EDUCATION OF A WANDERING MAN

## Cowpoke Horsesense

The fool with the least mind to share
is always tryin' to give you a piece of it.

## Saddlebag Bible

A prudent man keeps his knowledge to himself,
but the heart of fools blurts out folly.

—PROVERBS 12:23

## A Life Straight and True

Blessed is the real cowboy—
he rides straight and true,
he never listens to what cheaters
might try 'n put over on you.

He don't care for a slacker—
he puts stock in honest sweat;
no fancy, proud talkin' gambler
has dumb-suckered him yet.

Mostly he just pities a bitter man,
all sour 'n dried up in his heart,
who won't take time contemplatin'
what the Good Book talks about.

Picture this straight 'n' true cowman
like a spreading old oak tree—
he grows strong by life's river
no matter what his troubles may be.

Not so for cheaters, slackers,
and such;
they never last, or get what
they need.
Soon they're blowin' out of sight
like a lonely, busted-off tumble-
weed.

But the horseman with courage
and God's burnin' light in his soul
leaves a heritage of true honor
that'll never fade or grow old.

—BASED ON PSALM 1, BY DAVID KOPP

## Great Spirit

Almighty Father, hear my prayer.
Each range I cross, I know you're there.
Please watch each switchbacked trail I ride,
And through life's trials, be my guide.

Oh, God, who rules the earth and sky
And numbers bluebirds passing by,
Please help me hunt in every man,
The goodness put there by your hand.

Lord, make me gentle with the old
And when choice comes for good or gold,
Please give me wisdom, then, to seek
What's right before I act or speak.

Great Spirit, as you once were named,
Who ruled before this land was tamed,
When I must cross that Last Divide
Please grant me, Lord, a horse to ride.

You know I'll do just what I'm told,
But I'm not long on streets of gold
And harps, for me, can't match the song
Of nightguards as they ride along.

So when you're makin' up a crew,
To move celestial longhorns through
The heavens' rangelands up on high,
To that great trailhead in the sky

I'd rather pack my ol' war bag
An' be there, even riding drag,
Than makin' music on a lyre
Or be in some angelic choir.

Amen

—MIKE LOGAN, COWBOY POET, HELENA, MONTANA

*Cowboy Quote*

"I won't be wronged, I won't be insulted, I won't be laid a hand on. I don't do these things to other people and I require the same of them."

—JOHN WAYNE, IN "THE SHOOTIST"

*Cowboy Close-up*

**He Died with His Boots On**

*When this 91-year-old cowboy died alone, the world heard about it.*

CLARENDON, Texas—A man believed to have been the oldest working cowboy in Texas died the way he wanted, stretched out in the prairie grass with his boots on.

Thomas Everett Blasingame, 91, was found lying on his back by fellow cowhands at the JA Cattle Co. ranch near Clarendon in the Texas Panhandle.

"He was a good, kind man to everyone," his wife Eleanor said. "When he died, it was the first time I've ever seen a bunch of cowboys just crying. They were all devastated by his death."

*—From an obituary circulated worldwide by a news service after the death of Thomas Everett Blasingame, Sr. on Sept. 17, 1989*

Seven years later, that also is the assessment of his son, Thomas Blasingame, Jr., who grew up in the cow camps where his dad worked on the 320,000-acre ranch.

"My dad cowboyed all his life," his son says. "He wore chaps and spurs and wore a brush jacket that would turn the thorns. He wore a big Stetson and was particular with a saddle because he roped a lot of big, wild cattle. You want a stout one. Otherwise the tree in the saddle will break and will get you in trouble."

------------------------------------------------------------

## "I take care of my country, cattle, horses, and family, and I talk to God every day."

Tom, Sr. grew a mustache after his lip was cut by a spur during a fight, his son says. He didn't attend church but kept a Bible in camp. "One winter he got snowed in and read the whole Bible through twice." The story of Abraham was a favorite, his son says, because he was "the feller with all those ranches and cattle." His son recalls Tom, Sr. saying, "I take care of my country, cattle, horses, and family, and I talk to God every day."

As for taking care of problems, cowboys usually ironed out disputes themselves, sometimes by "whupping" one another. "You never heard no lawsuits in those days," Tom, Jr. says. "Nobody knew what a lawyer meant. If you messed up, you got fired and hit the road."

-----------------------------------------------------------------------

## Wanted:

A nice, plump, healthy, good-natured, good-looking, domestic and affectionate lady to correspond with. Object—matrimony. She must be between 22 and 35 years of age. She must be a believer in God and immortality, but no sectarian. She must not be a gadabout or given to scandal, but must be one who will be a helpmate and companion, and who will endeavor to make home happy. Such a lady can find a correspondent by addressing the editor of this paper. Photographs exchanged!

If anybody don't like our way of going about this interesting business, we don't care. It's none of their funeral.

—NOTICE IN THE **YUMA SENTINEL**, YUMA, ARIZONA, 1875

## Cowpoke Horsesense

A bad man with a fast gun never slept as well as a good man without one.

## Saddlebag Bible

A man of integrity walks securely,
but he who takes crooked paths will be found out.

—PROVERBS 10:9

- - - - - - - - - - - - - - - - - - - - - - - - - - - - - - - - - - - - - - - - - - - -

## The Friendliest Folks You Know

"A white pickup is coming the other way. I pull over so my left wheels ride the right-hand track, and she does the same. It's Glenna, our neighbor on the north, a widow who runs a place similar in size to our own. She gives us a broad grin and a big wave, which I return. If two pickups pass each other in the ruts of a wet clay road, and one has a 1900-pound bull trying to climb out over the rack and the other driver has just dropped his cigarette lighter and set fire to his pants—they wave."

—BOB ROSS, FROM IN THE KINGDOM OF GRASS

## Cowboy Fact

"Bury me next to Bill" was Calamity Jane's epitaph (Deadwood, South Dakota). The epitaph refers to Wild Bill Hickock, who is buried nearby. Calamity Jane was born Martha Jane Cannary Burke.

## Cowpoke Horsesense

"Big hat, no cattle."

—TEXAS SAYING FOR A MAN WHO PRESENTS HIMSELF AS MORE THAN HE IS

------------------------------------------------------------

## Racing Away with the Indian Horse

*A sense of justice on the frontier tended to work better with a sense of humor thrown in.*

"This is a tale of a buckaroo who decided to settle down. He opened a trading post.

"One day an Indian stopped and asked if the trader were interested in selling a fine-looking pinto tied to the hitching rail out front. 'Might be,' the trader told him. For the next half-hour the two haggled over the price.

"At last a deal was struck. The Indian paid and galloped away on the horse. The trader stood in front of the window watching and, when the wind-broken horse pulled up half a mile away because he could run no farther, the trader let out a belly laugh. He had fooled the Indian. He had got the best of the trade.

"Some time later the Indian and several members of his tribe arrived at the trading post. The owner sensed trouble but the Indians were friendly and at last the white man concluded the previous trade had been forgotten.

"One of the Indians was riding a bay horse with excellent conformation. The trader asked if it was for sale. The Indian shook his head no. This refusal only piqued the trader's interest and made him more determined. Finally he

**"The bay won the race going away and, of course, the trader insisted on buying the Indian horse."**

offered to race one of his horses against the bay, winner take all. The Indians held a quick council and agreed to the terms if the race would be from the trading post, around a lone juniper tree and back. The distance was slightly more than a quarter mile.

"The bay won the race going away and, of course, the trader insisted on buying the Indian horse. He knew several buckaroos who would pay top dollar for the animal. Eventually the Indians agreed to swap and they quickly departed with the trader's best horse and a new rifle.

"The trader gave the bay a close inspection and recognized something. A bucket of water and some elbow grease revealed the horse was the wind-broken pinto under a coat of brown dye."

—TOLD BY RICK STEBER, WESTERN FOLKLORIST, PRINEVILLE, OREGON

- - - - - - - - - - - - - - - - - - - - - - - - - - - - - - - - - - - - - - -

## Cowpoke Horsesense

You can't buy the kind of quality you can raise.

## Your Horse and Your Wife

"Give ninety percent and take ten percent on both sides. That's the way to get along with your horse or your wife."

—ROY ROGERS

## Keep Your End Up

*Advice to greenhorns who wanted to work on the High Plains trail drives*

"Keep your end up or turn in your string of horses. On the roundup, no soldiering goes; sick or well, it's hit yourself in the flank with your hat and keep up with the bunch or be set afoot to pack your saddle; there's no room in the chuck wagon for a quitter's blankets, and no time to close herd sick ones. So for heaven's sake don't start out unless you have the guts to stand it."

—N.R. DAVIS, COWBOY, CHEYENNE, WYOMING, 1870

## True Nobility

Who does his tasks from day to day
And meets whatever comes his way
Believing God has willed it so,
Has found real greatness here below.
Who guards his pot, no matter where,
Believing God must need him there,
Although but lowly toil it be,
Has risen to nobility.
For great and low there's but one test:
'Tis that each man shall do his best.
Who works with all the strength he can
Shall never die in debt to man.

—EDGAR GUEST, AMERICAN POET


## Saddlebag Bible

The glory of young men is their strength; of old men, their experiences.

—PROVERBS 20:29

## The Lord is My Saddle Pardner

My forty years' gatherin's
is a saddle and horse,
spurs and a bedroll,
a catchrope, of course.

I don't make much wages,
so the things that I own
are sure enough mine
'cause I can't get a loan.

Now folks might believe
I'd be lonesome out there
in those juniper breaks
where there's no one to share

the things that I hear
and the things that I see.
But I've got way more
than those folks'd believe

'cause the Lord is my saddle pardner.
We're never apart;
whenever I want
we can talk heart to heart.

And the Lord is also there
for each one of you—
if you've got a problem,
he knows what to do.

Just let him take charge
of all that we own;
with the Lord for our saddle
    pardner,
we're never alone.

—JON BOWERMAN, COWBOY POET AND
HORSE TRAINER, FOSSIL, OREGON

---

## Saddlebag Bible

His pleasure is not in the strength of the horse,
nor his delight in the legs of a man;
the Lord delights in those who fear him,
who put their hope in his unfailing love.

—PSALM 147:10-11

## Cowboy Lingo

*alkali*—alkaline salts that turn soil white or gray; found in dry basins and evaporated lake beds. The Great Salt Lake Desert is a large alkali flat.

*arroyo*—a gully

## Cowpoke Horsesense

An empty saddle is better than a mean rider.

## God Must Be a Cowboy at Heart

Campfire coffee from a tin cup in my hand
Shore warms the fingers when it's cold
Playin' an ol' guitar, a friend I understand
Sure smoothes the wrinkles in my soul.

Sleepin' in the moonlight, a blanket for a bed
It leaves a peaceful feelin' in my mind
Wakin' up in the morning with an eagle overhead
Makes me long to fly away before my time.

*chorus*
And I think God must be a cowboy at heart
'Cause he made wide open spaces from the start
He made grass and trees and mountains
and a horse to be a friend
and trials to lead ol' cowboys home again.

The night lights of big cities, they don't fit my style.
I just dream of the mountains when I'm there
'Cause the country's so pretty, it goes on and on for miles
And it takes away my troubles and my cares.

*chorus*
And I think God must be a cowboy at heart
'Cause he made wide open spaces from the start
He made grass and trees and mountains
and a horse to be a friend
and trials to lead ol' cowboys home again.

—SONG LYRICS BY DAN SEALS

## Cowboy Fact

*Will James*—cowboy novelist and illustrator from Montana, 1892-1942; a famous saying about him was, "He can't spell worth a cent."

*Will Rogers*—cowboy humorist and actor from Oklahoma, 1879-1935; a famous saying by him was, "All I know is what I read in the papers."

--------------------------------------------------------------

*Cowboy Close-up*

**You ride for the brand, or you don't ride here....**
*A rancher talks about loyalty, respect, and a workingman's code.*

Paul Chisholm, ranch manager
Monument, Eastern Oregon

T o get what he wanted growing up on Montana ranches, Paul Chisholm had to do what he hated—stay in school, and milk the cows. "The worst thing you could ever do is milk a cow. You're just a milkmaid for the rest of the crew. Milking is the worst," Chisholm says with conviction. "Now to keep a calf alive, any cowboy'd milk a cow in a snowbank...."

What Chisholm wanted was to be on horseback, doing a cowboy's work—maybe one day to have a spread of his own. Today he'll tell you that learning to make hard trade-offs was only his first lesson in ranch rules. "You get out there and do what's necessary," he says. "If it's 30 below and you're out there to help cattle, you better not be sittin' in your pickup looking at them through binoculars."

Times are changing, Chisholm says, and old-timers' honor can seem a thing of the past. But Chisholm can easily spell out the values he expects of himself and his ten-man crew every day:

"You better not let the sun come up without you being up."

"You ride for the brand, or you don't ride here. Loyalty matters when you're

-------------------------------------------------------------------

## Learning to make hard trade-offs was only his first lesson in ranch rules.

working side by side all day. You got a problem with someone, say it
to his face, not behind his back."

"Be responsible. If not, you or an animal could get killed."

"Do things right the first time, the first time you're told. Second chances
are hard to come by in this line of work."

"If something don't work, it's because you didn't make it work."

"Never ask a man to do something you wouldn't do yourself."

------------------------------------------------------------

## The Working Cowhand's Code

*Everyday good manners that working cowboys follow — and only rude dudes ignore.*

A cowboy:

- doesn't mess with another man's gear unless asked.
- doesn't tell another cowboy how to do something unless asked.
- doesn't pet, give commands to, or cuss another man's dog.
- knows which way the wind is blowing and never kicks dirt into another man's plate.
- doesn't cut in front of another rider on a trail, or crowd him from behind.
- never rides in front of the boss.
- doesn't wave when he meets another rider on a trail (it might scare the horses).
- never talks down to anyone (if one cowboy dismounts, the other one does too).
- never jumps his horse into a run if he has a long way to travel.
- never overworks or abuses his horse.
- always closes gates behind him.
- doesn't put his horse in the trailer until the boss tells him to.
- puts away his horse before he puts away his dinner.
- removes his spurs before entering a house or pickup truck.

—FROM STEPHEN BULL, COWBOY OBSERVER AND PART-TIME BUCKAROO, BURNS, OREGON; AND MICHELE MORRIS IN **THE COWBOY LIFE**.

## Some Things Do Change

Cowboys invited to a ranch house for dinner should show no interest in the women of the household, or even an appreciation for their hospitality, except by eating heartily at their table.

—COWBOY ADVICE FROM THE 1880s

## Saddlebag Bible

A man of knowledge uses words with restraint and a man of understanding is even-tempered.

—PROVERBS 17:27

# A Cowboy's Prayer

----------------------

Oh Lord, I've never lived where churches grow.
    I love creation better as it stood
That day you finished it so long ago
    And looked upon your work and called it good.
I know that others find you in the light
    That's sifted down through tinted window panes,
And yet I seem to feel you near tonight
    In this dim, quiet starlight on the plains.

…I thank you, Lord, that I am placed so well,
    That you have made my freedom so complete;
That I'm no slave of whistle, clock, or bell,
    Nor weak-eyed prisoner of wall and street.
Just let me live my life as I've begun.
    Make me a pardner of the wind and sun,
And I won't ask for a life that's soft or high.

Let me be easy on the man that's down;

    Let me be square and generous with all.

I'm careless sometimes, Lord, when I'm in town,

    But never let 'em say I'm mean or small!

Make me as big and open as the plains,

    As honest as the hoss between my knees,

Clean as the wind that blows behind the rains,

    Free as the hawk that circles down the breeze!

Forgive me, Lord, if I sometimes forget.

    You know about the reasons that are hid.

You understand the things that gall and fret;

    You know me better than my mother did.

Just keep an eye on all that's done and said,

    And right me, sometimes, when I turn aside,

And guide me on the long, dim trail ahead

    That streches upward toward the Great Divide.

—CHARLES BADGER CLARK, 1920

# ACKNOWLEDGEMENTS

Grateful acknowledgment is given for permission to quote from the following:

"The Lord is My Saddle Pardner," lyric by Jon Bowerman. All rights reserved.

*Out West* by Dayton Duncan (Viking Penguin Books, New York, NY, 1987).

*Out West: The Cowboys* by William Forbis and the Editors of Time-Life Books (Time-Life Books, Inc., Alexandria, VA, 1973).

"That's Why I'll Never Be Anything But a Cowboy," lyric by Jack Hannah (Great American Cowboy Music—The Sons of the San Joaquin, c/o Scott O' Malley & Associates, Colorado Springs, CO). All rights reserved.

*The Oregon Desert* by E. R. Jackman and R. A. Long (The Caxton Printers, Caldwell, ID, 1964).

*Steens Mountain* by E. R. Jackman and John Scharff (The Caxton Printers, Caldwell, ID, 1967).

"Driftin' On" and "Close the Gate," self-published poems by Everett G. Jones. All rights reserved.

Excerpts from "Home" by William Ketteridge, reprinted from *Owning It All* (Graywolf Press, St. Paul, MN).

*Blue Highways* by William Least Heat Moon (Little, Brown and Company, New York, NY, 1982).

"Calf" and "Great Spirit," from *Men of the Open Range & Other Poems* by David Michael Logan (Buglin' Bull Press, 32 S. Howie, Helena, MT, 1993). All rights reserved.

"The Cowboy Life" and "Resist All," from *The Cowboy Life in Short and Poems* by J'Wayne "Mac" MacArthur (self-published, 1988). All rights reserved.

"Little Things," by Wallace McRae, from *Between Earth and Sky: Poets of the Cowboy West*, edited by Anne Heath Widmark (W. W. Norton & Company, New York, NY, 1995). Used by permission of the author. All rights reserved.

"God Must Be A Cowboy At Heart" words and music by Dan Seals (Pink Pig Music, Morningstar Management, Hendersonville, TN). All rights reserved.

*Pan Bread 'N Jerky* by Walter L. Scott (The Caxton Printers, Caldwell, ID, 1968).

"The Trade," from *Cowboys, Tales of the Wild West Series* by Rick Steber (Bonanza Publishing, Box 204, Prineville, OR, 1988).

"Reminiscences of a Rimrocker," by Emmet White and Annette White Parks (*Oregon Historical Quarterly*, Portland, OR, fall, 1984).

--------------------------------------------------------------------

Grateful acknowledgement is also given for use of the following:

*A Taste of Ranching: Cooks and Cowboys*
    by Tom Bryant and Joel Bernstein
*Cowboys and the Wild West* by Don Cusic
*Cowboy Culture* by David Dary
*The Ultimate Horse Book* by Elwyn Hartley Edwards
*Cowgirls* by Ronnie Farley
*Working Cowboys* by Douglas Kent Hall
*Cowboy Wisdom* by Terry Hall
*The Way West: Art of Frontier America* by Peter Hassrick
*The Education of a Wandering Man* by Louis L' Amour
*Songs of the Cattle Trail and Cow Camp,* by John A. Lomax
*In the Kingdom of Grass* by Margaret MacKichan and Bob Ross
*Cowboy: The Enduring Myth of the West* by Russell Martin
*The Cowboy Life* by Michele Morris
*Voices and Visions of the American West* by Barney Nelson
*The Sagebrush Ocean* by Stephen Trimble
*The Working Cowboy's Manual* by Fay E. Ward
*The Virginian* by Owen Wister